Anna Eleanor Roosevelt

Anna Eleanor Roosevelt

★★★★★★★★★★★★★★★★★★★

1884–1962

BY DAN SANTOW

CHILDREN'S PRESS®
A Division of Grolier Publishing
New York   London   Hong Kong   Sydney
Danbury, Connecticut

Consultants: ALLIDA BLACK, PH.D.
George Washington University

LINDA CORNWELL
Coordinator of School Quality and Professional Improvement
Indiana State Teachers Association

Project Editor: DOWNING PUBLISHING SERVICES
Page Layout: CAROLE DESNOES
Photo Researcher: JAN IZZO

Visit Children's Press on the Internet at:
http://publishing.grolier.com

Library of Congress Cataloging-in-Publication Data
Santow, Dan.
    Anna Eleanor Roosevelt, 1884–1962 / by Dan Santow
       p. cm. — (Encyclopedia of first ladies)
    Includes bibliographical references and index.
    Summary: A biography of the wife of the thirty-second president, a woman devoted to
helping others and working for peace.
    ISBN 0-516-20694-X
    1. Roosevelt, Eleanor, 1884–1962—Juvenile literature. 2. Presidents' spouses—United
States—Biography—Juvenile literature. [1. Roosevelt, Eleanor, 1884–1962 2. First ladies.
3. Women—Biography] I. Title II. Series
E807.1.R48S26 1999
973.917'092—dc 21   98–45238
[B]   CIP
                                  AC

Table of Contents

Anna Eleanor Roosevelt

CHAPTER ONE

The Beginning of a New Beginning

* * * * * * * * * * * * * * *

When an aide crept quietly to Eleanor Roosevelt's chair and whispered that the First Lady had an urgent phone call from the White House, she stood as silently as she could and softly walked out of the room. Eleanor was at a benefit, one of hundreds she had attended during her years as First Lady, and didn't want anyone to become alarmed. When she answered the phone, she was told she was needed back at the White House immediately.

"I did not even ask why," she later said. "I got into the car and sat with clenched hands all the way to the White House. In my heart I knew what had happened,

* * * * * * * * * * * * * * *

Eleanor Roosevelt arriving at a benefit shortly before Franklin's death

but one does not actually formulate these terrible thoughts until they are spoken."

This was the beginning of the end of a long road for Eleanor Roosevelt. And while she hardly wished for it to end this way, she had never really been comfortable being First Lady. She had been First Lady for twelve years—a whole generation of children had known no other. With each new election, she had secretly hoped it would be her husband's last. Franklin Delano Roosevelt (FDR) was elected president in 1932 and 1936. After these two terms, each time the oppor-

tunity to run again presented itself, Eleanor had secret misgivings about becoming First Lady for yet another four years.

Before the last election, in 1944, she had again been apprehensive. But these had been difficult times, and difficult times often call for courageous decisions. Franklin was particularly good at making them. Eleanor recognized this, even if such a decision seemed to work against her own best interests.

When Franklin first ran for president in 1932, Eleanor was certain even then that if he won she would

Franklin Roosevelt waving his hat to a crowd in Detroit, Michigan, during the 1932 presidential campaign

Term Time

✮ ✮

Franklin Delano Roosevelt was elected to the presidency four times between 1932 and 1944, serving in the office for twelve years. (Had he lived to complete his fourth term, he would have been president for sixteen years.) At the time, the Constitution did not limit the number of terms a president could serve, but Roosevelt was the first and only man to serve for more than two. Until then, presidents by tradition declined to run for more than two terms. Thomas Jefferson, the third president, set the example early when he refused to run for a third time, saying that three terms would be like holding the office for life. While monarchs might serve for a lifetime, that was not appropriate for the elected president of a democractic nation. FDR reasoned, however, that under the grave circumstances of World War II, stability in the presidency would be important. In response to FDR's long reign, Congress put forward a constitutional amendment declaring that "no person shall be elected to the office of the President more than twice. . . ." The Twenty-second Amendment became law in 1951.

The Roosevelt family is all smiles on election night, November 3, 1936, after the returns showed that Franklin had won a second term as president.

lose her independence, that she would be doing nothing but hosting teas and fancy-dress balls.

"I was happy for my husband," recalled Eleanor, ". . . and I had implicit confidence in his ability to help the country in a crisis. . . . But for myself I was deeply troubled. As I saw it, this meant the end of any personal life of my own."

Eleanor had seen her aunt Edith Roosevelt's life change when her uncle Teddy Roosevelt was elected president, so she had some idea what lay ahead. "I cannot say that I was

Eleanor's aunt, Edith Roosevelt

Former president Theodore Roosevelt was Eleanor's uncle, her father's older brother.

President Franklin Delano Roosevelt and First Lady Eleanor Roosevelt leaving church on Easter, 1941

pleased at the prospect," she said. As the day of Franklin's first inauguration drew closer, Eleanor's fear grew stronger. At one point, a reporter asked her what sort of First Lady she hoped to be. "There isn't going to be any First Lady," she said. "There is just going to be plain, ordinary Mrs. Roosevelt. And that's all."

By 1940, Franklin had served two terms and, though there was no law against running more than twice, no president had ever done so. Franklin had served his country well, however,

and though Eleanor longed for independence, she knew by 1939 that World War II would necessitate Franklin's third campaign. She feared that a different president would not be able to handle depression and war as deftly as FDR would. "My own personal opinion—and not as the wife of a president—is that except in extraordinary circumstances we should stick to our traditions," Eleanor had said. Even though that tradition was two terms, these were indeed extraordinary circumstances.

It wasn't that she didn't like being First Lady—if nothing else, she was certainly used to it by now! But even with all the pomp and circumstance, with chauffeurs and servants, and people who were anxious to hear what she had to say, it could be frustrating.

Yet Eleanor had always managed to escape the glare occasionally. She lived as First Lady in the White House, but when she was able to get away, she lived in Hyde Park, New York. Franklin had built a stone cottage for her on the estate where his childhood home still stood. She named the cottage Val-Kill, after a nearby brook, and went there as often as she could. It was Val-Kill that she really considered home, and the small town of Hyde Park her hometown.

"I am always given the reputation of constantly being on the move," Eleanor said in one lecture. In fact, she added, a woman had once remarked that she did not see very much evidence that Eleanor ever stayed at home. Actually, Eleanor said, "I believe very strongly in deep roots in some piece of ground . . . some place that carries your memories and associ-

Eleanor chatting with a group of young music students in 1939

ations of many years. All of us need deep roots. We need to feel there is one place to which we can go back, where we shall always be able to work with people whom we know as our close friends and associates, where we feel that we have done something in the way of shaping a community."

By almost every estimation, Eleanor had done just that, but on a grander scale. Instead of having done

Eleanor addressing the Association of Foreign Press Correspondents at a 1940 luncheon in New York

Eleanor sitting behind Franklin in the backseat of a presidential campaign car

"something in the way of shaping a community," as she had said, she had done much to shape the entire nation. She had fought hard for the rights of women and for the rights of African Americans, among others.

Once, in a half-joking mood, she described what it was like to be First Lady. "Always be on time," she said. "Never try to make any personal engagements. Do as little talking as hu-

manly possible. Never be disturbed by anything. Always do what you're told to do as quickly as possible. Remember to lean back in a parade, so that people can see your husband. Don't get too fat to ride three on a seat. Get out of the way as quickly as you're not needed."

Franklin had run for a third term as president, and had won. World War II was beginning to rage at the time of this election, and four years later, the war was winding down. Franklin had been a brilliant president during his

World War II began on September 1, 1939, when Germany invaded Poland.

President Roosevelt in Bridgeport, Connecticut, during the presidential campaign of 1944

third term. By 1944, victory was very near.

Sensing this, and setting aside her personal feelings about living in the White House for four more years, Eleanor championed Franklin's decision to run once again. "I think he faced the fact, five years ago, that if he had to go on in office to accomplish his work, it must shorten his life, and he made that choice," she said. "If he can accomplish what he sets out to do, and then dies, it will have been worth it. . . ."

Though Franklin had started to slow down during his third term, the fourth campaign seemed to energize him. He campaigned vigorously, partly because Eleanor told him he must if he wanted to win. Eleanor noticed that he "improved visibly in strength and resilience." That strength paid off, too, and allowed him to win the election.

Now, barely five months after his and Eleanor's triumph, much of the strength he had shown during the

President Roosevelt giving a radio broadcast during the 1944 presidential campaign

The house in Warm Springs, Georgia, where Franklin Roosevelt died on April 12, 1945

election was sapped. While Eleanor was at the benefit in Washington, Franklin was at his vacation home in Warm Springs, Georgia, sitting for a portrait. At one point, he put his hand to his head and collapsed. It was 3:35 on the afternoon of April 12, 1945. The president was dead.

Returning from the benefit to the White House a short time later, Eleanor was escorted in and given the news. She immediately cabled her four sons, all of whom were in the armed forces. "Darlings," she wrote to them, "father slept away this afternoon. He did his job to the end as he would want you to do."

President Roosevelt was sitting for this portrait by Elizabeth Schoumatoff when he died.

Lieutenant John Roosevelt

Lieutenant Commander Franklin Roosevelt Jr.

Colonel James Roosevelt

Colonel Elliott Roosevelt

18

She then summoned Harry Truman to the White House to tell him of the president's death. Stunned, the vice president asked, "Is there anything I can do for you?" To which Eleanor responded, "Is there anything *we* can do for *you?* For you are the one in trouble now."

Then she left for the 800-mile (1,287-kilometer) trip to Warm Springs to accompany Franklin's body back by train to the capital. On the train ride home, Eleanor said, "I lay in my berth all night with the window shade up looking out at the countryside he had loved and watching the faces of the people at stations, and even at the crossroads, who came to pay their last tribute all through the night."

Finally back at the White House, Eleanor asked to be alone with the coffin, and to open it for a few minutes. "Mrs. Roosevelt stood at the casket gazing down into her husband's face," said a White House usher who stood guard. "Then she took a gold ring from her finger and tenderly placed it on the president's hand. She straightened, eyes dry, and she left the room. The coffin was never opened again."

A weeping Graham Jackson played the accordion at FDR's funeral in Hyde Park.

A huge crowd gathered on the White House lawn after the announcement of President Roosevelt's death.

The flag-draped casket of the late president moves toward the burial site on the Roosevelt estate at Hyde Park, New York.

After the burial service, Mrs. Roosevelt left the gravesite escorted by her daughter Anna Roosevelt Boettiger and her son, Brigadier General Elliott Roosevelt, who is carrying the flag that draped the casket.

This was it then, she thought, the end. "The story is over," she told a reporter.

Though she had been voted one of the most admired women in the world and was known around the globe as a force for peace in the world, in some ways she still saw herself as the shy, awkward little girl she had been. And she couldn't believe that after Franklin's death anyone would care about what she said or thought. She felt, she said, "the sorrow of all those to whom the man who now lay dead, and who happened to be my husband, had been a symbol of strength and fortitude."

At his funeral, the only piece of jewelry she wore was a gold pin Franklin had given her on their wedding day in 1905.

"About the only value the story of my life may have is to show that one can, even without any particular gifts, overcome obstacles that seem insurmountable," Eleanor said toward the end of her life. "That, in spite of timidity and fear, in spite of a lack of special talents, one can find a way to live widely and fully."

CHAPTER TWO

Call Me Eleanor

☆ ☆ ☆ ☆ ☆ ☆ ☆ ☆ ☆ ☆ ☆ ☆ ☆ ☆ ☆

Unlike many other First Ladies before and after her, Eleanor Roosevelt's fame is not based solely on her years living in the White House as the president's wife. Calvin Coolidge's wife, Grace, for instance, is hardly remembered for much other than that she had been First Lady in the 1920s.

This was not the case with Eleanor Roosevelt. By the time she reached the White House, she was already an internationally known activist. She had lived in Albany, New York, when her husband was the state's governor, and in Washington, D.C., during World War I when he was assistant secretary of the navy. She

☆ ☆ ☆ ☆ ☆ ☆ ☆ ☆ ☆ ☆ ☆ ☆ ☆ ☆ ☆

Unlike Eleanor Roosevelt, who was an internationally known activist, Grace Coolidge (shown here with her husband President Calvin Coolidge) was remembered mainly for the fact that she had been First Lady during the 1920s.

had written newspaper and magazine articles and had lectured and traveled widely. After her husband's death, despite her initial feelings that she would soon be forgotten, she continued to speak out on behalf of those less fortunate than she was. As a delegate to the United Nations, she chaired the committee that wrote the Universal Declaration of Human Rights.

Profile of America, 1884: America Shows Off

☆ ☆ ☆ ☆ ☆ ☆ ☆ ☆ ☆ ☆ ☆ ☆ ☆ ☆ ☆ ☆ ☆ ☆ ☆ ☆

When Eleanor Roosevelt was born, America was changing from a farming country to an industrial one. Even isolated communities around the 38 states and 9 territories were now connected by railroads and phone lines. As the "Wild West" slipped into history, cities rose rapidly on the landscape. Americans learned they could make money through invention and industry, and many did.

Middle-class and wealthy Americans delighted in showing off their success with excess. They bought expensive homes, clothing, and other possessions. Fashionable women upholstered themselves in yards of elegant silks and satins and wore bustles—frames to support even more fabric—at their backs. More than ever before, complicated dressmaking and luxurious materials made an expensive gown reflect its wearer's stature and wealth. Houses took on strange and elaborate shapes, too, as towers, turrets, and carved ornaments became popular. Entertainments flourished. As wages went up and working hours went down, a growing middle class had more money and more time to enjoy the theater, the circus, sporting events, museums, and symphonies. The first roller coaster opened at Coney Island in New York. In baseball, Moses Fleetwood Walker became the first African American in the major leagues as a catcher for the Toledo, Ohio, team. An African-American jockey, Isaac Murphy, won the Kentucky Derby aboard Buchanan, trained by an African-American trainer.

Some Americans had little to show off. Eager to share in the prosperity, immigrants from Europe arrived here by the thousands. But factory work was hard on them, and so was a city life of poverty. Even children had to toil long hours to add to family incomes. An average worker made about $400 per year in 1884, while it took about $600 to live decently. Industrial workers felt "dehumanized" and banded together into labor unions to press for their rights. African Americans began to feel the sting of new laws that encouraged segregation. Out West, as settlers, ranchers, and farmers took over the last Native-American lands and nearly wiped out the buffalo, the end of traditional tribal life drew near.

In Washington, D.C., Grover Cleveland was elected to his first term. In December, the 555-foot (169-meter) Washington Monument was completed with the addition of its topmost stone. Begun in 1848, the simple marble shaft must have seemed in some ways a monument to a simpler America.

Her extraordinary life spanned eight decades, from before the turn of the century when travel by horse and buggy was the only way to go, through her husband's four elections as president, two world wars, and into the early 1960s, when jet travel was common. All along the way, Eleanor made her mark, despite feeling that she was never doing quite enough.

"Duty . . . was perhaps the motivating force of my life, often excluding what might have been joy or pleasure," she said. "I looked at everything from the point of view of what I ought to do, rarely from the standpoint of what I wanted to do. . . . I was never carefree."

Anna Eleanor Roosevelt—she hardly ever used her given first name, Anna—was typical of many other First Ladies in only one way: She was born into wealth and privilege. And yet, for all the money and mansions and nannies and fancy parties, she did not have a happy childhood.

Eleanor and Franklin vacationing at Warm Springs in 1929, when Franklin was governor of New York

These pictures show Eleanor as a child (left), during girlhood, as a young woman, and during her later years.

Eleanor Roosevelt's life spanned eight decades, from the horse-and-buggy era of the late 1800s (above) to the jet age of the early 1960s.

Both her parents came from wealthy families and were used to lives of leisure, travel, and entertainment. Her tall and handsome father, Elliott, was interested mainly in playing polo, attending horse shows, and fox-hunting.

Her mother, Anna, was one of the most beautiful women Eleanor had ever seen. "[I was] grateful to be allowed to touch her dress or her jewels or anything that was part of the vision."

The elegant and beautiful Anna hoped that her daughter Eleanor, born

Eleanor's mother and father, Anna Hall and Elliott Roosevelt, younger brother of Theodore

All in the Family

✴ ✴

The Roosevelts are an old and remarkable American family. As fifth cousins once removed, Eleanor Roosevelt and Franklin Delano Roosevelt were both descended from the original family member to arrive in America several generations before they were born. Claes Martenszen van Rosenvelt came from Holland to the Dutch settlement at New Amsterdam (now New York City) in the 1640s. In the following years, his descendants helped to build America as farmers, patriots, merchants, bankers, businessmen, and philanthropists. Politics, too, played a role in the Roosevelt family. Claes' two grandsons, Johannes and Jacobus, both had great-great-great-grandsons who became presidents: Eleanor's uncle Theodore (her father's brother), a Republican, became the twenty-sixth president of the United States, and Franklin, a Democrat, the thirty-second. Through the years, the Roosevelt men married women from prominent families as well. Eleanor's mother, for instance, was a direct descendant of Robert R. Livingston, who administered the oath of office to the first president, George Washington.

Above: Eleanor with her brothers Elliott (left), and baby Hall

Left: Eleanor and her brother Elliott about 1890

New York, U.S.A.

✶ ✶

Anna Eleanor Roosevelt was born in New York, the Empire State, in 1884. New York stretches from the Atlantic Ocean west to the Great Lakes and north to Canada. While lovely farm and forestlands cover most of its 49,112 square miles (127,200 square kilometers), the great metropolis of New York City occupies its southernmost corner. At the end of the 1800s, New York, like all American cities, was growing fast. During Eleanor's childhood there, it was a city of contrasts. The small island of Manhattan, the heart of New York City and only 22 square miles (57 sq km) in size, supported over a million people by the 1880s, from the very wealthy to the desperately poor. Families like Eleanor's lived in the most fashionable "silk stocking" neighborhoods; not far away, the poorest immigrants crowded into slums. In some areas, the population density reached 334,000 people per square mile. With no regular garbage collection, a poor sewage system, choking air pollution, and other unsanitary conditions, city streets bred disease, stench, and pests. About the same time, however, New Yorkers saw the founding of the Metropolitan Opera, the establishment of a world-class symphony, and the first telephone and electrical service. In 1886, the city dedicated the Statue of Liberty, symbol of the land of opportunity—and contrast.

on October 11, 1884, would be the same. Eleanor, however, turned out to be far from graceful—she wore a brace to correct curvature of the spine—and was certainly not beautiful. Though she had shining blue eyes, she also had an overbite and a receding chin. She was always too tall for her age and slightly gawky. This didn't sit well

with Anna, who could be very disapproving. "I knew it as a child senses these things," Eleanor said. "She tried hard to bring me up well so that my manners would compensate for my looks, but her efforts only made me more keenly conscious of my shortcomings."

Once, when her mother was entertaining a guest, Eleanor stood in the archway, too shy to enter the room. "She's such a funny child, so old-fashioned, that we always call her 'Granny,'" Eleanor's mother said to her friend. Even Eleanor had to admit she was not the happiest child. "I was a solemn child," she recalled, "without beauty and painfully shy and I seemed like a little old woman entirely lacking in the spontaneous joy and mirth of youth."

The only real joy and satisfaction she did have as a child really came from her relationship with her father. He was always ready to laugh and have fun. Eleanor remembered as a child once being dressed up and invited down to do a little dance for her father and his friends, who applauded when

Elliott Roosevelt with his children, Elliott (left), Hall (on his knee), and Eleanor

Six-year-old Eleanor especially loved the time spent in Venice during the Roosevelt family vacation in Europe.

she finished. Her father picked her up high in the air and twirled her around.

"With my father I was perfectly happy," she recalled. "He was the one great love of my life as a child and in fact, like many children, I have lived a dream life with him, so his memory is still a vivid, living thing to me."

Elliott Roosevelt had a dark side, as well, however. He often drank too much and forgot to come down to dinner. Sometimes he forgot to come home at all and stayed away for days at a time.

When Eleanor was six years old, her entire family went to Europe for three months in the hope that Elliott might be able to stop drinking if he were away from home. For Eleanor, this was a time of pure delight. She spent days on end with her father and remembered particularly their stay in Venice, Italy, where Elliott acted like a gondolier, "singing with the other boatmen, to my intense joy. I loved his voice, and above all, I loved the way he treated me," Eleanor said. "I never doubted that I stood first in his heart."

That may have been true, but Elliott failed to stop drinking and his occasionally thoughtless behavior, even to Eleanor, failed to change. Once he took her and three of their fox terriers for a walk near their townhouse in Manhattan. When they neared his club, he told Eleanor to wait while he went in for a moment, that he would be right back. An hour passed, then two, then three, then four, then five, then six! All the while, Eleanor stood patiently waiting, holding onto the dogs' leash. Finally, Elliott returned— but he was so drunk that he had to be carried out. The doorman ended up taking Eleanor home.

About the time Eleanor turned eight, Elliott was in Virginia, once again trying to stop drinking. Anna contracted diphtheria and became very ill, and Elliott started for home. "I can remember standing by a window when cousin Susie told me that my mother was dead," Eleanor said. Anna was only twenty-nine years old. "Death meant nothing to me, and one fact wiped out everything else. My father was back and I would see him soon."

Without a mother to raise the children, Elliott sent Eleanor and her brothers to live with Anna's mother, their Grandmother Hall. There,

After their mother died, Eleanor and her brothers were sent to live with their Grandmother Hall at Oakridge (right), in Tivoli, New York.

Eleanor is shown here at the age of ten, about the time her father died.

Eleanor studied with tutors but mostly just waited for visits or letters from her father. She lived in a dream world, then, she said, "in which I was the heroine and my father the hero. Into this world I withdrew as soon as I went to bed and as soon as I woke up in the morning and all the time I was walking or when anyone bored me."

Even her dream world was shattered when she was ten. Her father, drunk and depressed, tried to kill himself by jumping out of a window. Soon

Alcoholism

★ ★

Eleanor's father and several of her other relatives, including her brother Hall, suffered and died from a disease called alcoholism. In her father's day, doctors understood little about the disease, and most people believed that those who drank too much simply lacked the willpower to stop. Now, we know that some people have a body chemistry that causes a physical addiction to alcohol that makes it hard for them to control their drinking. Because alcohol is a poison, the consumption of too much wine, beer, or hard liquor can destroy the body's organs. Clearly, too much alcohol is never good for anyone, and alcoholics often suffer from liver failure and other deadly diseases. Today, experts estimate that 18 million people are afflicted with alcoholism in the United States alone. Although the nature of the disease is better understood and accepted, no drug will cure it. The best treatment still seems to be to learn to stop drinking completely with the help of a support group such as Alcoholics Anonymous.

Eleanor (with bicycle) and her Aunt Maude (in a horse-drawn cart) are shown here at Grandmother Hall's estate.

afterward, he had a seizure and at the age of thirty-four, he, too, died. "My aunts told me," Eleanor recalled, "but I simply refused to believe it, and while I wept long . . . I finally went to sleep and began the next day living in my dream world as usual. . . . From that time on . . . I lived with him more closely, probably, than I had when he was alive."

Though her father had died young, and before that had often treated his family poorly, Eleanor refused to be moved. She loved him unconditionally in a way her affections for her mother could not match. "[My father] dominated my life as long as he lived," Eleanor wrote in her memoirs, "and

was the love of my life for many years after he died."

"Poor child," her grandmother wrote of Eleanor, "[she] has had so much sorrow crowded into her short life she now takes everything very quietly. The only remark she made was, 'I did want to see father once more.'"

Her father had not only been everything warm and wonderful to her, but he had been the one person who held her in high esteem. He had made it clear that he expected more from her than just good manners or a pretty face, but in addition expected her to be an upstanding person. As one historian wrote, Eleanor's father, despite his alcoholism, ". . . gave her

Eleanor and her brother Hall

Eleanor Roosevelt at the age of fifteen, shortly before she left for Allenswood

the ideals that she tried to live up to all her life by presenting her with the picture of what he wanted her to be—noble, studied, religious, loving, and good."

Despite Elliott's love and influence, however, his death served only to make an already insecure little girl even more so. "I was not only timid, I was afraid," Eleanor said, "afraid of almost everything, I think: of mice, of the dark, of imaginary dangers. . . ."

Her grandmother ran a very strict household, with a time and place for everything. Once lights were out for the evening, for instance, they were out, period. Eleanor, an avid reader, would hide books beneath her mattress so she could read late into the night without her grandmother knowing. As far as Eleanor was concerned, her grandmother raised her "on the principle that 'no' was easier to say than 'yes.' "

By the time Eleanor turned fifteen, her grandmother decided to send her

An Allenswood class picture showing the female students in their uniforms of straw hats, white ruffled blouses, and ankle-length skirts

away to a boarding school outside of London called Allenswood. Up to this point in her life, she had been educated by private tutors—she spoke French before she even knew English!—so Allenswood would be her first taste of formal education. It would prove a turning point in her life.

This was the first time Eleanor was truly on her own, away from the constraints of an unhappy and tragedy-filled childhood and the grim atmosphere of her grandmother's mansion. Her new headmistress, Mademoiselle Marie Souvestre, was a strong-willed woman and an excellent teacher with an instinct for bringing out the best in her students. In Eleanor, she found an avid student, a young girl lacking in confidence but brimming with enthusiasm for learning and doing.

Mademoiselle Souvestre had so much influence on Eleanor that she even got her newest student to stop biting her fingernails!

Allenswood was a strict school. All the girls wore uniforms of straw hats, white ruffled blouses with striped neckties, and dark ankle-length skirts—and they were allowed only three ten-minute baths a week. However, the school allowed Eleanor a freedom she had never before known.

At Allenswood, Eleanor studied

English literature, history, algebra, French, German, Italian, and Latin. Though she took three years of piano and one of violin, artistic endeavors did not come easily to her. "I struggled over the piano and was always poor," she commented later in life. "I could not draw, much less paint. I envied every good actress, but could not act!" She worked hard and even accomplished things she would never have predicted, such as earning a place on the field hockey team, "one of the proudest moments of my life," she wrote.

It was at Allenswood that Eleanor first became interested in philosophy and politics, both of which were then thought to be men's interests. For Eleanor, they would eventually become lifelong passions.

As much as Eleanor was affected by the powerful Mademoiselle Souvestre, she in turn was taken with Eleanor. "All that you said when she came here of the purity of her heart, the nobleness of her thought has been verified by her conduct among people who were at first perfect strangers to her," she wrote to Eleanor's grandmother.

"I have found she influenced others in the right direction."

For Eleanor, Allenswood was the place where for the first time in her life she was admired and respected for being something other than the daughter of wealthy and beautiful parents. Here, she was cherished and honored for being the intelligent, thoughtful, caring person she was.

Allenswood, she said, started her on the way to self-confidence. "I have spent three years here," she wrote, "which have certainly been the happiest years of my life."

Mademoiselle Souvestre was to be one of the most important people in Eleanor's life. Aside from her positive influence during daily life at Allenswood, she opened Eleanor's eyes to an entirely different world from the one she had been brought up in. Through their summer travels, Souvestre introduced Eleanor to settlement work. For the first time, she was exposed to immigrants and the poverty-stricken slums in which they lived. The indelible impressions were to color Eleanor's activities throughout the rest of her life.

CHAPTER THREE

Friendship, Then Marriage

☆ ☆ ☆ ☆ ☆ ☆ ☆ ☆ ☆ ☆ ☆ ☆ ☆ ☆ ☆ ☆

When Eleanor sailed from Europe after finishing her years at Allenswood, she was heading not only for home, but toward a new life. Though she continued to live with her grandmother, she was now a young woman with some freedom to come and go and do as she pleased. It was 1902, and women of her wealth and background were expected to make a debut, or formal entrance, into society; attract a rich, important husband; and settle down to a life of charity fund-raising, leisure, and running a large home filled with servants.

Though Eleanor did make her debut, reluctantly,

☆ ☆ ☆ ☆ ☆ ☆ ☆ ☆ ☆ ☆ ☆ ☆ ☆ ☆ ☆ ☆

Eleanor taught in a settlement house in the dirty, crowded Lower East Side of New York City.

none of the trappings of society particularly appealed to her. In Europe, having formed more serious interests than many of her girlhood peers in New York, Eleanor instead became interested in volunteer work. In New York, like many girls in her circle, she did join an organization called the Junior League, whose members organized fund-raising events to help the poor. Eleanor, though, was eager to do more than just raise money, she wanted to help in a more meaningful way.

She was assigned to teach little girls in a settlement house on the Lower East Side of New York. At first, she later recalled, "the dirty streets, crowded with foreign-looking people, filled me with terror, but the children interested me enormously. I still remember the glow of pride that ran through me when one of the little girls said her father wanted me to come home with her, as he wanted to give me something because she enjoyed her class so much."

Eleanor's thirst for learning about the world beyond her grandmother's front steps was difficult to satisfy. Her work with poor immigrant children, and seeing how they sometimes were forced to work long hours under terrible conditions, led her to join the Consumers' League, an organization trying to better conditions for working women.

Just as she had been unfamiliar with minorities, she was also unaccustomed to women who worked for a living. But now she started to visit factories and department stores and saw women working twelve to fourteen hours a day for six days a week, and

Houses of Hope

✫ ✫

The "settlement house movement" began in the 1880s to provide some quality of life in America's poor inner cities. By 1900 in New York City, more than 2.5 million people lived and worked in the shadow of the skyscrapers in the most miserable slums. And still they came. Irish, Germans, Jews, Russians, Italians, and other immigrants crowded into New York and sister cities by the hundreds of thousands hoping to find work. Instead, they worked to find hope, and neighborhood settlement houses tried to help. Run mostly by well-educated middle-class women, they gave the newcomers a haven where they could learn, play, socialize, and even wash. Children of all nationalities attended kindergarten and women studied nutrition and American cooking. Boys took "manual training," working with tools and learning trades. At the University Settlement House at Rivington and Eldridge Streets on New York's Lower East Side, Eleanor taught calisthenics and "fancy dancing." For the children, such play and learning time must have been a welcome relief from their otherwise bleak existence. While

The University Settlement House

many activities encouraged immigrants to celebrate and preserve their native traditions, others were designed to teach them about American culture and customs to help them get along better in their newly adopted land.

Eleanor was shocked to discover that children of four or five years of age were doing piecework for hours on end in New York City tenements.

In the late 1800s and early 1900s, women worked twelve to fourteen hours a day for six days a week at very little pay in the sweatshops of New York and other large cities.

earning only $6 for a week's work. When she visited a factory where artificial flowers and feathers were made, she was shocked by the conditions. She visited her first sweatshop and walked up the steps of her first tenement. She saw children of four or five years of age sitting at work tables until they dropped with fatigue. "I was frightened to death," she said, "but this was what had been required of me and I wanted to be useful."

She was only nineteen at that time, but she had seen at firsthand the horrible way some people were treated and lived. She recalled having "painfully high ideals and a tremendous sense of duty . . . entirely unrelieved by any sense of humor or any appreciation of the weakness of human nature." She thought of herself as a curious mixture of extreme innocence and unworldliness with, she

Formal dating in the early 1900s was governed by very strict rules of conduct.

Nineteen-year-old Eleanor worked as a volunteer in New York City's Lower East Side.

said, "a great deal of knowledge of some of the less agreeable sides of life."

During this time of expanding her interests in the world outside what was expected from her, she was exploring the dating world as well. For though she was unlike other young women in many ways, she too wanted a husband and family.

Relationships between men and women back then were far different than they are today. They were more formal, stiffer, and less spontaneous.

43

Eleanor in 1903, after she and Franklin had formed a serious relationship

Women simply did not show interest in a man unless he showed some interest first. "There were few men who would have dared to use my first name, and to have signed oneself in any other way than 'very sincerely yours' would have been not only a breach of good manners but an admission of feeling which was entirely inadmissible," Eleanor recalled. "You never allowed a man to give you a present except flowers or candy or possibly a book. To receive a piece of jewelry from a man to whom you were not engaged was a sign of being a fast woman, and the idea that you would permit any man to kiss you before you were engaged to him never even crossed my mind."

But there was one man with whom Eleanor began a serious relationship—her fifth cousin once removed, Franklin. Though they had met on a few family occasions in the past—her father had been his godfather—they did not know each other well as children. In the summer of 1902, however, they met one day on the train while Eleanor was traveling to her grandmother's country house and Franklin,

By 1903, Franklin Delano Roosevelt was falling in love with his fifth cousin, Eleanor Roosevelt.

Franklin (circled) was a member of Harvard's Hasty Pudding Club.

a junior at Harvard, was going upstate. They hadn't seen each other since a family Christmas party a few years earlier, and this happy meeting sparked new interest in them both.

At first, they formed a friendship, but soon romance blossomed between them. Franklin invited Eleanor to his family's country house for weekends where, at twilight, they would sit on the porch overlooking the Hudson River and read poetry out loud to each other. He invited her to dances and football games at Harvard, and when

Franklin (standing) is shown here with his parents, James and Sara Delano Roosevelt, in 1900, when he was attending Harvard College.

with her. She was different from the other girls he knew. Most of them were interested in little but clothes and parties. "If you ever find me leading this type of life," Eleanor told Franklin, "stop me, for it's not the way to happiness." Once, when she took Franklin to visit a poor, sick child she knew from her volunteer work, he left as shocked as she had once been by

they were apart, they wrote love letters to each other almost daily.

"Though I only wrote last night," Eleanor wrote to Franklin, "I must write you just a line this morning to tell you that I miss you every moment and that you are never out of my thoughts dear for one moment. . . . I am so happy. Oh! So happy and I love you *so* dearly." Before going to bed at night, she would kiss his letters.

He, in turn, always enjoyed being

A 1904 picture of Franklin and Eleanor at Sara Roosevelt's cottage on Campobello Island, New Brunswick, Canada

Remembering Springwood

✫ ✫

Franklin Delano Roosevelt (FDR) was born in an upstairs bedroom at his family's Hyde Park estate, Springwood, and the place stayed in his blood until his death. Purchased by FDR's father in 1866, the house nestles in the woods along the Hudson River. FDR spent much of his life at Springwood. There he played as a boy and cultivated his love of stamp collecting and naval history. He launched his political career from Springwood in 1910, and ever after, the mansion bustled with activity. During his four presidencies, FDR retreated to Springwood 200 times for work and relaxation. When the British king and queen visited in 1939, the Roosevelts held an old-fashioned American picnic in their honor, complete with hot dogs. Over the years, Franklin planted nearly a half-million trees on the property. In 1940, he added a library to house his papers and collections. He even deeded the house to the government so that all Americans could enjoy it as a National Historic Site. But, while Franklin adored Springwood, Eleanor was never entirely comfortable there. She always felt it to be the domain of FDR's controlling mother, Sara. Nine months before his death, Franklin confessed that "All that is within me cries out to go back to my home on the Hudson River." And so he did. Both he and Eleanor are buried in the rose garden at Springwood in Hyde Park.

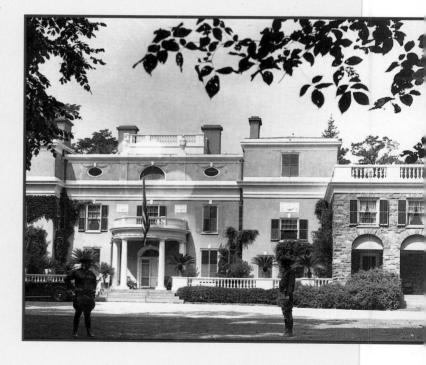

Franklin took this picture of Eleanor in a gondola in Venice, Italy, during their honeymoon.

Eleanor spent a quiet hour in a Greek garden during her European honeymoon.

such a sight. "My God," he said, "I didn't know people lived like that!"

One weekend, when Franklin and Eleanor were visiting her brother at boarding school in Massachusetts, Franklin proposed. "When he told me that he loved me and asked me to marry him, I did not hesitate to say yes, for I knew that I loved him too," she said. He was twenty-one years old and she was nineteen, filled with "the urge to be a part of the stream of life."

Franklin, for his part, told his mother, Sara, that he was "the happiest man in the world, likewise the luckiest." Sara, who was very close to

Franklin, was alarmed at the news of their engagement. As far as she was concerned, no one could replace her in Franklin's heart, and she begged them to wait a year before announcing their engagement.

Despite the delay, they did marry, on St. Patrick's Day, 1905. Dressed in a satin gown covered in Brussels lace just like her mother's and grand-mother's dresses had been, she walked down the aisle on the arm of her uncle, Theodore Roosevelt, who was the president of the United States at the time. "Well, Franklin," the president said after they were pronounced husband and wife, "there's nothing like keeping the name in the family!"

Eleanor's wedding was another milestone in her life. But little did she know then that, as a pair, she and Franklin would accomplish so much as individuals, helped along by one another's interests, tenacity, and ambitions.

Franklin and Eleanor are pictured here in San Remo, Italy, during their honeymoon.

CHAPTER FOUR

From Lady of the House to First Lady

✦ ✦ ✦ ✦ ✦ ✦ ✦ ✦ ✦ ✦ ✦ ✦ ✦ ✦ ✦

As sophisticated as Eleanor had become since returning from school in Europe, she was still in many ways a woman of her times. She had only a passing interest in what she thought of as matters best left to men, such as politics, for instance. On her honeymoon, when someone asked her a question about the structure of the U.S. government, she didn't know the answer. She was even against the right of women to vote. "I had never given the matter serious thought," she said, "for I took it for granted that men were superior creatures and knew more about politics than women did."

✦ ✦ ✦ ✦ ✦ ✦ ✦ ✦ ✦ ✦ ✦ ✦ ✦ ✦ ✦

Eleanor and her daughter Anna on a 1907 Campobello Island vacation

Eleanor and Franklin's first three children (from left), Elliott, James, and Anna

Her life as a young wife, in fact, was developing into just what she had always feared it might. "I suppose I was fitting pretty well into the pattern of a fairly conventional, quiet, young society matron," she wrote many years later. "I was beginning to be an entirely dependent person. . . . I was not developing any individual taste or initiative. I was simply absorbing the personalities of those about me and letting their tastes and interests dominate me."

She began to have children as well—five boys, one of whom died in infancy, and a girl, whom she named Anna after her mother. "For ten years I was always just getting over having a baby or about to have another one," she said, "so my occupations were considerably restricted."

Eleanor was uncomfortable as a mother. Because she had had an unhappy childhood, she felt unsure of herself with the children. "It did not come naturally to me to understand

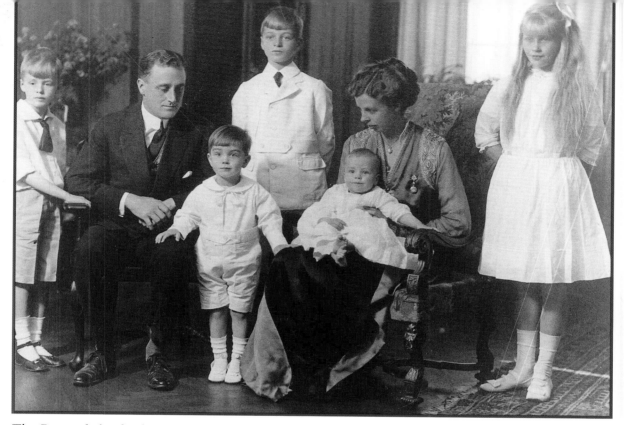

This Roosevelt family photograph, taken in 1916, shows Franklin and Eleanor with their four sons and their oldest child, Anna (right)

little children or to enjoy them," she said. "Playing with children was difficult for me because play had not been an important part of my own childhood."

Like her own mother before her, she had maids to do much of the work. "For years I was afraid of my nurses," Eleanor said, " . . . who ordered me around quite as much as they ordered the children."

In addition to feeling cowed by the children's nurses, Eleanor felt equally pressured by Franklin's domineering mother, Sara.

When Eleanor's first children arrived, Sara scolded her about continuing to do volunteer work, saying it could bring disease into the household, so Eleanor quit. Sara had told me that "I had no right to go into the slums or into the hospitals, for fear of

Sara Delano Roosevelt (1854–1941)

✫ ✫

Franklin's mother was one of eleven children born to Warren and Catherine Delano. "Sallie" grew tall and stately. Her bearing reflected her refined upbringing in a privileged household. Her father made his money trading in China, and in 1862, his family joined him there. For eight-year-old Sara, the 128-day ocean voyage by sailing ship must have been quite an adventure. The Delanos returned from China after the Civil War to their gracious home along the Hudson River in New York. In 1880, Sara married James Roosevelt. The marriage united two old New York

families whose ancestors had arrived in the seventeenth century. Though James was twice Sara's age, their marriage was a happy one. When James died in 1900, Sara was forty-six, and she lavished all her affection on their only child, college-aged Franklin. Sara Delano Roosevelt was in every way a classic "matriarch," or ruling mother. Though their relationship was close, Eleanor always felt dominated by her mother-in-law. Ironically, the polio that disabled FDR's legs helped Eleanor "stand on her own two feet" since she was at last able to assert herself with Sara and gain the confidence to grow and achieve on her own.

Franklin's mother, Sara Delano Roosevelt, looking fondly at a baby picture of her son

bringing disease home to my children."

Sara even rented a town house in New York City for Eleanor and Franklin and their growing family. She furnished it and hired a cook, butler, and maid. She even bought pots and pans for them! Eventually, Sara built a house for them right next door to her own, with sliding doors that opened

between her living room and theirs. There was little privacy.

One night, Franklin returned home from his job on Wall Street and found Eleanor crying. "When my bewildered young husband asked me what on earth was the matter with me," Eleanor recalled, "I said I did not like to live in a house that was not in any way mine, one that I had done nothing about and which did not represent the way I wanted to live."

It was 1910, and Franklin, too, was living a life he wasn't comfortable with. He decided to enter politics and run for the New York state senate. He

President Woodrow Wilson appointed Franklin D. Roosevelt (right, shown with Admiral William S. Sims) assistant secretary of the navy in 1913.

won, which meant the family would be moving to Albany, the capital. "I listened to all his plans with great interest," Eleanor wrote, but " . . . it never occurred to me that I had any part to play."

Moving to Albany, of course, meant that Eleanor would not only be getting away from Sara, but that she would have a chance to get back into the community. As a politician's wife, she said, "I was beginning to get interested in human beings and I found that almost everyone had something interesting to contribute to my education." Within three years, they moved again, this time from the state capital to the nation's capital, when Franklin was appointed assistant secretary of the navy under President Wilson.

The seriousness of the times—World War I began in 1914—meant that Eleanor could stop doing many of the things she found dissatisfying, such as hosting teas and dinners. "I found myself spending three days a week in a canteen down at the railroad yards," she later said, "one afternoon a week distributing yarn for the Naval League, two days a week visiting the naval hospital, and contributing whatever time I had left to the Navy Red Cross and the Navy Relief Society." She was so busy that her shyness was disappearing very quickly. For the first time since going to school in Europe, Eleanor began to feel confident in her own abilities. "I loved it," she recalled. "I simply ate it up."

While her life as a politician's wife continued to shine, trouble was brewing within the confines of her family. One day in 1918, with Franklin in bed

World War I: Fast Facts

WHAT: The "Great War," the "War to End All Wars," the first truly global conflict

WHEN: 1914–1918

WHO: The Central European Powers, including Austria-Hungary and Germany, opposed the Allied Powers, including Britain, France, and Russia. The United States entered the war on the Allied side in 1917.

WHERE: The Central Powers invaded Serbia, Romania, Russia, Belgium, France, and Italy. Fighting extended into the Atlantic Ocean and the Mediterranean Sea.

WHY: European disputes over land, economics, religion, and leadership boiled over in 1914 when Austrian archduke Francis Ferdinand was assassinated on a visit to Serbia. Austria declared war on Serbia, and other European nations joined in. The United States got involved largely because German submarine warfare disrupted commerce in the North Atlantic Ocean.

OUTCOME: The Central Powers fell to the Allied Powers in 1918, and an armistice was signed on November 11. The map of Europe was redrawn and the League of Nations was founded to settle international disputes. Ten million soldiers, including 116,500 Americans, had died.

"Knit Your Bit"

✫ ✫

As the country entered World War I, Americans pitched in as Eleanor did, volunteering to serve soldiers on their way to Europe at makeshift canteens in railroad stations. Many knitted socks for soldiers and sewed pajamas for the wounded. To conserve supplies, food, and energy, Americans endured endless rationing, cutting back on everything from coal to butter. Patriotic citizens observed "heatless, meatless, and wheatless" days. Since Germany led the world in producing fabric dyes, color disappeared from American clothing. Steel went into guns and tanks instead of women's corsets. Women wore lower heels in an effort to provide leather for military harnesses and belts. Cloth was conserved by eliminating outside pockets on men's suits. Youngsters hooted at anyone thoughtless enough to drive their cars on gasless Sundays, while diligent motorists hitched horses to their bumpers.

suffering from pneumonia, Eleanor was unpacking his luggage when she came across a bundle of letters—love letters. They were to Franklin, from her own secretary, Lucy Mercer.

"The bottom dropped out of my own particular world," Eleanor said. She confronted Franklin and offered him a chance for divorce. Franklin's friend and adviser Louis Howe was firmly against this idea, arguing that it would ruin his political career.

Instead, Franklin stopped the affair and all but begged Eleanor's forgiveness. This Eleanor was willing to do, but their marriage would never again be the same.

"The truth of the matter is that a deep and unshakable affection and tenderness existed between them," said their son James. That may have been true, but their relationship was no longer one based on shared romance, but instead became a shared partnership of two like-minded people with similar goals and ambitions. "I have the memory of an elephant,"

Eleanor told friends years later, recalling this difficult time in her life. "I can forgive but I can never forget."

Worse, when the family was on vacation on Campobello Island off the coast of New Brunswick, Canada, in 1921, Franklin complained of a chill and went to bed early. He awoke the next day with a high fever and a great deal of pain; he couldn't stand or move his legs. Fearing the worst, they called a doctor, who diagnosed polio. Franklin would forever more be paralyzed from the waist down, unable to walk or stand without the help of heavy metal leg braces.

A President with Polio

✫ ✫

When polio struck, Franklin Roosevelt decided not to let it get the better of him. The disease is caused by a virus that paralyzes the muscles and makes it difficult or impossible to move. Though he never walked by himself again, Franklin worked hard at swimming and physical therapy to strengthen his upper body. He looked so fit that most Americans never knew he had no use of his legs. Roosevelt did everything he could to keep it that way because he was afraid that the disease would make him appear weak or unfit for the presidency. During his carefully planned public appearances, he wore stiff braces on his legs, stood by leaning on stools, and occasionally walked a few steps with considerable help. He designed his own wheelchairs, sawing the legs off wooden kitchen chairs and adding wheels. These homemade chairs were less obvious and more maneuverable. He even had a car outfitted so that he could drive. By the time FDR was deciding to run for a fourth term, however, his health was worsening. To keep his heart condition from the public, photographers were discouraged from taking close-up pictures. Nonetheless, pictures taken near the end of World War II reveal a sickly and tired FDR. For the first time ever, Roosevelt apologized for sitting through a speech, saying that his heavy leg braces made it difficult to stand. He died three months later.

As a result of the Lucy Mercer affair, her experiences as a wartime volunteer, and now this, Eleanor had grown considerably. She had been forced by circumstances to stand up for herself, to act on her own, and to develop a new set of friends outside her marriage. When Sara urged her son to retire to the family's country estate in Hyde Park, Eleanor did just the opposite. She fought for Franklin to stay as involved in life as possible. She disagreed with Sara so strongly over this, and was so angry, that once she even blocked the sliding doors between their houses to keep Sara out. "Mama and I have had a bad time," Eleanor wrote in her diary. "I should be ashamed of myself and I'm not."

Franklin's illness, Eleanor said, "made me stand on my own two feet in regard to my husband's life, my own life, and my children's training."

Franklin hadn't retired to Hyde Park, or anywhere else for that matter. In fact, by 1928, after practicing law in New York since the family's return, he was once again bored. And, once again, he decided to run for office— this time for governor of New York.

Franklin and Eleanor in Hyde Park in 1928

Eleanor Roosevelt, wife of the new governor of New York, greets visitors to the Executive Mansion in Albany on December 31, 1928.

A Home of Her Own

☆ ☆

While Franklin had his beloved Hyde Park estate Springwood, Eleanor had Val-Kill. Franklin understood that Eleanor needed a hideaway of her own, so in 1925, he designed a stone cottage to be built on a favorite picnic spot on the Springwood grounds. Eleanor named it for the creek that flowed nearby and invited two close friends to live in the cottage. She would visit whenever she could. With characteristic energy, Eleanor and her friends—women she had met during the course of her political activities—decided the next year to add another building to house a small furniture-making business that they called Val-Kill Industries. They hoped to provide jobs for local people who might otherwise leave the area. For ten years, Val-Kill Industries trained workers in the art and craft of furniture making. They turned out replicas of early American designs. The little factory closed in 1936, and Eleanor converted it into a home for herself. Cozy and snug, she decorated the cottage simply as was her style and then covered the walls with photos of the people she "collected." After Franklin's death, Val-Kill became Eleanor's permanent, and much loved, home for the rest of her life.

Members of the Roosevelt family gathered around the Christmas tree at the Executive Mansion on December 27, 1929.

He won, of course, and again the family moved to Albany.

As far as Eleanor was concerned, Franklin's polio, however tragic, worked to his advantage.

"Franklin's illness proved to be a blessing in disguise," Eleanor wrote, "for it gave him strength and courage he had not had before. He had to think out the fundamentals of living and learn the greatest of all lessons—infinite patience and never-ending persistence."

More independent than ever now, Eleanor began to travel and make speeches condemning segregation in the South. She even began working four days a week as a teacher of literature, drama, and American history at a girls' school called Todhunter. She also traveled around the state with Franklin inspecting state hospitals and

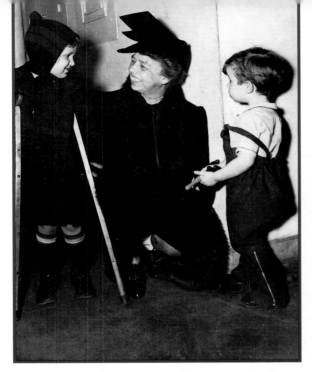

As the wife of the governor, Eleanor traveled the state inspecting hospitals (above) and prisons.

FDR shaking hands in Nebraska during his 1932 campaign for the presidency

prisons. While he would be driven around the grounds, it was Eleanor who would actually go inside. She was eager to do it and to learn as much as she could from the experience. Eleanor also became politically active in the state of New York and in the Democratic Party. She led the Dutchess County delegation to the 1922 Democratic state convention, and after her first speech, *The New York Times* called her a "highly intelligent and capable politician."

According to one historian, it was during this time when her husband was governor that she "became famous not as FDR's wife, but as a major political force to be reckoned with."

In 1932, Franklin ran for president. Wasn't she afraid that a strenuous campaign would affect her husband's health? one reporter asked. "If polio didn't kill him," Eleanor responded, "the presidency won't."

However, she wasn't sure it would

Democratic candidate for president Franklin Roosevelt (front left) with his family at Hyde Park during the 1932 campaign

not harm her. She had been an active First Lady of the state of New York and did not want to lose that. When Franklin won the election, her fears only worsened. "My zest for life is . . . gone for the time being," she told a friend that spring. "If anyone looks at me I want to weep. . . . It makes me feel like a dead weight and my mind goes round and round like a squirrel in a cage. I want to run, and I can't, and I despise myself. I can't get away from thinking about myself. Even though I know I'm a fool, I can't help it!"

The day after the election, Eleanor went to teach her class at Todhunter. "We think it's grand to have the wife of the president for our teacher," a student said when she gave Eleanor a present in front of the entire class. Eleanor looked down at her and smiled. "I don't want you to think of me that way," the new First Lady said. "I'm just the same as I was yesterday."

FDR and Eleanor reading a congratulatory
telegram from Herbert Hoover on election night

This formal photograph of new First Lady Eleanor
Roosevelt was taken in 1932.

Former president
Herbert Hoover
(right front), who
had lost the 1932
election to FDR,
was in attendance
as Franklin took the
oath of office as
president on
January 20, 1933.

CHAPTER FIVE

Breaking Traditions

As First Lady, Eleanor began breaking traditions almost immediately. At first, she changed only little things: for instance, she ran the White House elevator herself and greeted White House guests as they entered instead of waiting until they were all there and making a grand entrance. When the servants began to move furniture around after she moved in, she pitched in and helped. Later, she was the first First Lady to drive her own car, though she refused to allow Secret Service agents to follow her. They did give her a pistol for protection. "I [took] it and learned how to use it," she wrote. "I do not mean by this that I am an

expert shot. I only wish I were." Still, she believed that no one would ever hurt her, even though people tried.

"I simply can't imagine being afraid of going among [Americans] as I always have," she said, "as I always shall."

She also took a flight from Washington to Los Angeles, the first time a First Lady had flown across the country. The trip instantly galvanized the nation and made it take notice.

"Here is what she takes the medal for," said one thrilled letter-to-the-editor in *The New York Times.* "Out at every stop, day or night, standing for photographs by the hour, being interviewed, talking over the radio, no sleep. And yet they say she never showed one sign of weariness or annoyance of any kind, no maid, no secretary—just the First Lady of the land on a paid ticket on a regular passenger flight."

The president was pleased with his wife's adventures. "My missus goes where she wants to!" he said.

Eleanor changed some of the bigger traditions, as well. Until Eleanor, First Ladies rarely, if ever, spoke to the press. In fact, Lou Hoover, the previous First Lady, never spoke to the press unless it was about the Girl Scouts, an organization she supported.

Eleanor quickly changed that. Initially, she started holding weekly press conferences, talking to the press about what was on her mind, answering questions as thoughtfully as she could. She even held her first press conference two days before the president held his! There were differences between Eleanor's press conferences and her husband's, however. At Eleanor's press conferences, for instance, only women were allowed in. "God's gift to newspaperwomen," one female reporter called the new First Lady.

Eleanor didn't hesitate to talk about controversial, serious things, such as sweatshops—she called for the end to child labor and for people to buy from stores with decent working conditions. "Sometimes I say things which I thoroughly understand are likely to cause unfavorable comment in some quarters, and perhaps you newspaperwomen think I should keep them off the record," Eleanor said at one press conference. "What you don't understand is that perhaps I am making these statements on purpose to arouse controversy and thereby get the topics talked about and so get people to thinking about them."

Neither the women-only press conferences nor the flight across the country were done expressly to gain publicity or to set a tone, but they did both nonetheless. They said to the country: "Watch out, you've got a new First Lady unlike any of her predecessors." Of course, anyone who knew her understood that she would not be the sort of First Lady who concentrated on entertaining foreign dignitaries and redecorating the White House. Though she hadn't asked to become First Lady,

Eleanor Roosevelt was the first First Lady to fly across the country.

During the depression, hungry, unemployed people stood in breadlines in almost every big city.

once she moved into the White House, she took advantage of her position. She believed, she said, that she could use the power of her new role to fight for the greater good.

Franklin, after all, had been elected in the midst of the third year of the Great Depression. Millions of people had lost all their money and millions more were unemployed. There were breadlines in almost every big city. Banks were closing daily. Eleanor realized that the country's problems were as much emotional as economic. She vowed to do as much as she could to turn things around. She wrote that the greatest enemy was "fear of an uncertain future, fear of not being able to meet our problems, fear of not being equipped to cope with life as we live it today." That was a fear, she thought, the First Lady could help combat.

Though Eleanor could hardly have known then the span of time in which she would live in the White House, her twelve years there were filled with action. She traveled constantly. She visited slum dwellers in Puerto Rico and sharecroppers in southern cotton fields. She would surprise the people running government relief programs, "often managing to arrive without advance notice so that they could not be polished up for my inspection." She proposed programs and legislation.

In August 1934, during one of Eleanor's cross-country trips, she visited the impoverished coal-mining

Opposite: On one of her many trips, the First Lady visited children in the slums of Puerto Rico.

The Crash of 1929 and the Great Depression

✫ ✫

In the fall of 1929, the American economy appeared hale and hearty. Investors in the stock market could hardly believe their good fortune as the value of their stocks shot higher and higher. Americans everywhere followed the market with great excitement as it soared. More and more people began to speculate, or buy stocks hoping that their value would increase. Some overextended themselves by borrowing money to buy more stocks. The prospect of easy profits obscured the warning signs that an economic crisis was looming. Most of America's money was concentrated in the hands of a wealthy few. The prices for farm products fell and farmers lost money. Rural banks failed because farmers couldn't pay off their loans. Ordinary consumers didn't make enough money to buy all the goods that businesses were producing. Finally, disaster struck when the stock market "crashed." Investors who had borrowed money began to sell their stocks to cover their debts. Stock prices nose-dived. On October 29, 1929—known as Black Tuesday—panicked investors sold more than 16 million shares of stock for much less than they had paid. Fortunes disappeared in minutes. The crash ruined banks, businesses, and individuals and triggered the worst depression in American history.

On one of her trips, Eleanor visited local musicians in a rural area of Virginia.

town of Scotts Run, West Virginia. Her report to the president about the miserable conditions there affected him so much that he created an Appalachian resettlement project. Federal money was used to build houses, schools, and craft shops in a new community, which was called Arthurdale.

Eleanor traveled so much that the president himself couldn't always keep track of her. Once, Eleanor went to Baltimore to inspect a prison, but Franklin didn't know that. When he called for her, an aide said she was "in prison." "I'm not surprised," Franklin said, "but what for?"

Though he might not always have known where she was, he knew when she returned. They had a ritual: On the night she got back, they always had dinner together so she could tell him what she had seen and learned while she was away. "I became, as the years went by," she recalled, "a better reporter and a better observer. I found myself obliged to notice everything."

And that she did. As she saw more and more how unfairly African Americans were treated, for instance, she began to speak out. "When a person holds deep prejudice," she said, "he

A formal portrait of President Franklin Delano Roosevelt

gets to dislike the object of his prejudice. He uses it as an excuse for the fact that there is something unworthy in himself."

In 1938, during Franklin's second term, Eleanor attended a meeting of the Southern Conference for Human Welfare in Birmingham, Alabama. When she arrived, she wanted to sit with her friend, African-American educator Mary McLeod Bethune. She was told that she couldn't do that because black people had to sit on one side of the room, whites on the other. Eleanor refused to obey, and when the police told her it was the law, she took a chair and placed it smack in the center of the aisle.

Two months later, the Daughters of the American Revolution (DAR), a group of women whose ancestors had fought in the Revolutionary War, refused to rent space to the great African-American opera singer Marian Anderson. Eleanor was a member of the DAR, but when she heard the news, she resigned from the organization. She then worked with the National Association for the Advancement of Colored People (NAACP) to help organize an outdoor concert for Anderson on the steps of the Lincoln Memorial. Possibly in part as a result of the publicity Eleanor had received when she quit the DAR, more than 75,000 people attended the concert to show their support. Anderson opened with the song "America" and ended

More than 75,000 people attended Marian Anderson's concert on the steps of the Lincoln Memorial.

73

Marian Anderson (1897?–1993)

★ ★

Marian Anderson gave her first concert at a church fund-raiser as a little girl. Then called the "Baby Contralto," Anderson would go on to become the "voice one hears once in a century." But the path was not easy. She was born in Philadel-

phia where her father sold ice and coal and her mother worked as a domestic. Her loving family was very active in the church, where Marian did a lot of singing as a youngster. Anderson loved music and everyone knew she had a talent, but finding enough money for voice lessons was difficult. In 1929, because racial restrictions prevented her from studying and touring in the United States, her church and several kind voice teachers raised enough money for her to travel to Europe to study and perform. Audiences loved the classical works and African-American spirituals that she sang so beautifully. Her popularity grew, and she gave 92 recitals in 70 cities in one year. Throughout her career, she performed for adoring audiences around the world. Regardless of her lovely voice, however, she still encountered prejudice because of her skin color. While the incident with the DAR was a bleak moment in her career, the most triumphant came in 1955, when Marian Anderson became the first African American to perform at New York City's famous Metropolitan Opera.

the evening with the song "Nobody Knows the Trouble I've Seen."

During World War II, Eleanor worked hard to end discrimination in the army, eventually securing two directives issued from the War Department—one that wouldn't allow recreational areas to be segregated and another that said that government-owned-and-operated buses had to be available to all soldiers, regardless of race. She also successfully fought to open the Army Nurse Corps to African-American women.

Eventually, she not only spoke to the reporters at her press conferences, she joined them when, in 1936, she started writing a folksy newspaper column called "My Day." In it, she described what she was doing and thinking and told stories about herself, her family, and her friends. She also gave her opinions on issues of the day. She often appeared on radio and wrote nearly 500 magazine articles. One article was called "Women Must Learn to Play the Game As Men Do," in which she urged more women to get involved in politics. She gave seventy

Eleanor dictating a draft of her newspaper column, "My Day," to her secretary, Malvina Schneider

speeches a year and wrote twenty-three books. It seemed that Eleanor was just about everywhere at once.

Not all of Eleanor Roosevelt's work and opinions were appreciated. During one of her husband's campaigns, his opponent passed out buttons that said, "We don't want Eleanor either." She was called "Madame President" and "Empress Eleanor." When she was asked why she couldn't stay home with her husband "and tend to her knitting as an example for other women to follow," she said, "If I could be worried about mud-slinging, I would have been dead long ago. . . . Almost any woman in the White House during these years of need would have done what I have done."

Even that didn't stop the barbs, however. "If you have any influence with the president," someone wrote Franklin's secretary, "will you please urge him to muzzle Eleanor Roosevelt and it might not be a bad idea to chain her up—she talks too . . . much."

The president didn't think so at all. He valued her opinion—and she could be relentless in offering it to him. Sometimes it seemed he listened

This full-length, formal photograph of First Lady Eleanor Roosevelt was taken in December 1933.

Franklin argue *her* side of the issue, point by point, with the American ambassador to England.

"Without giving me a glance or the satisfaction of batting an eyelash, he calmly stated as his own the politics and beliefs he had argued against the night before!" she wrote later. "To this day I had no idea whether he had simply used me as a sounding board, as he so often did, with the idea of getting the reaction of the person on the outside, or whether my arguments had been needed to fortify his decision and to clarify his own mind."

Eleanor and Franklin discussed the depression, the war, and politics often. After all, she was his wife. "You don't just sit at meals and look at each other!" she once said. Sometimes, though, things got heated. At dinner one night when the president and Eleanor were arguing over some issue, their daughter Anna interrupted by saying, "Mother, can't you see you're giving father indigestion?"

Life in the Roosevelt White House was always hectic, what with both Franklin and Eleanor leading such complex, busy lives. It wasn't unusual

to her more than even she thought. One night, they had a discussion of some issue about which they disagreed. The next day, she heard

The ever-expanding Roosevelt family always gathered at the White House for Christmas celebrations. In this 1939 photograph, the president is in the center and Eleanor is at the far left.

for them both to be traveling at the same time but not together.

When they were both home, they spent as much time with their children as possible, "with all of them talking at once," according to one of Franklin's advisers. The First Lady would raise an issue "and her sons at once began to wave their arms in the air and take issue with her. . . . The president joined in at intervals, but he wasn't president of the United States on that occasion—he was merely the father of sons who had opinions of their own. They interrupted him when they felt like it and all talked at him at the same time. It was really most amusing."

The Roosevelt children, all of whom married and divorced numerous times while their parents still lived in the White House, were always welcome, said Eleanor, "with their joys or with their sorrows. We cannot live other people's lives and we cannot make their decisions for them."

Of all the children, it was Anna with whom she was the closest. They shared a deep love of each other formed after years of what was basically a pretty rocky relationship. The tension ended when Eleanor was reading a story to her sons and she broke down crying. The pressure of motherhood, it seemed, was taking its toll. According to one historian, Eleanor "flung herself on her bed and sobbed shamelessly for hours."

"This outburst of mine," said Eleanor many years later, "had a good result so far as Anna and I were concerned. She saw that I was not cold and unfeeling after all. And she poured out her troubles to me, saying she knew she had been wrong in thinking I did not love her. It was the start of an understanding between us."

In some ways, it was exactly that— forging understandings among people—at which Eleanor excelled. During Franklin's third run for the presidency, the Democratic National Convention was held in Chicago. Franklin hadn't campaigned for the

Anna, the oldest of the Roosevelt children and the only girl, became very close to her mother.

nomination, thinking that as the Second World War loomed, he would win without much of a fight. But the delegates to the convention were unhappy with his choice for vice president, and Franklin became nervous. He asked Eleanor to fly to Chicago and speak to the delegates on his behalf.

After all, he thought, the people loved her just as she was. In his second campaign, four years before, she had traveled with him. At every campaign stop, people would clamor for her to come out. "If she failed to appear on the platform," one reporter noted, "they shouted for her until she did appear, and they cheered her just as heartily as her husband, sometimes more heartily." More recently, Franklin knew, another newspaper had called her "a force on public opinion, on the President, and on the government . . . the most influential woman of our times."

Who better, then, to make a speech in his favor to a mob of angry delegates? Eleanor, who was at her house in Hyde Park on vacation, had been following the convention on the radio. When Franklin first asked her to go, she was unsure if she should, saying that a woman's place in politics wasn't on the stage but in the background "smoothing the way" for her husband. But Franklin needed her and Eleanor flew to Chicago.

The audience fell silent as she reached the podium to speak. Whomever won the election, she said, would bear a "heavier responsibility, perhaps, than any man has ever faced before in this country. . . . You cannot treat it as you would an ordinary nomination in an ordinary time. . . . So

Eleanor's speech to the Democratic National Convention in 1940 saved the nomination for Franklin.

each and every one of you who give him this responsibility, in giving it to him assume for yourselves a very grave responsibility. . . . You will have to rise above considerations which are narrow and partisan. This is a time when it is the United States we fight for."

No one spoke, no one moved. They only listened, enthralled by her every word. Then a huge cheer rumbled through the crowd, with wild applause and stamping feet.

Franklin, who had heard the

Eleanor pins a shamrock on FDR's lapel on their thirty-ninth wedding anniversary, March 17, 1941.

The president and Eleanor attending a formal evening function

speech on the radio, was so thrilled that he had her plane stopped on the runway as she was starting to return home just to tell her how proud he was. When he accepted the nomination later in the week, he said that since he was calling on young men to serve the country he could hardly refuse when the people were calling upon him to do the same. Eleanor had saved his nomination and made it possible for him to lead the country through war and to victory.

The war years, though, were the toughest. With men marching off in record numbers, and in many cases not returning at all, Eleanor decided that one way she could be useful was by traveling to where they were stationed to boost morale and to let the servicemen know they were loved and appreciated.

For security reasons, the plans for her trip to England after the 1940 election were kept secret. Yet she was met there at the train station by King

World War II: Fast Facts

WHAT: The second great global conflict

WHEN: 1939–1945

WHO: The Axis Powers, including Germany, Italy, and Japan, opposed the Allies, including Britain, France, and the USSR. The United States entered the war on the Allied side in 1941 after the bombing by Japan of Pearl Harbor in Hawaii.

WHERE: Fighting raged throughout the Pacific Ocean and in the Atlantic as well as from Scandinavia to North Africa, and deep into the Soviet Union.

WHY: Chancellor Adolf Hitler set out to make Germany the most powerful country in the world, and began by invading his European neighbors. Japan, Italy, and Germany pledged support to one another in 1940. When the United States declared war on Japan after the attack on Pearl Harbor in 1941, Germany and Italy declared war on the United States.

OUTCOME: The war ended in stages. Germany surrendered in May 1945. Japan surrendered after the United States dropped two atomic bombs there in August. More than 400,000 American troops died in battle; about 17 million on both sides perished.

George VI and Queen Elizabeth. She made inspections, toured, lectured and—according to one very tired reporter who followed her—walked "50 miles through factories, clubs, and hospitals." She viewed the destruction of London by Nazi bombs, inspected a parachute battalion and even got to sit in a bomber's cockpit. "I found I'm very fat for a pilot's seat," she joked afterward.

In 1943, she asked to tour the South Pacific, including Hawaii, Australia, New Guinea, New Zealand, and many smaller islands. Eventually, she visited 400,000 soldiers and traveled 23,000 miles (37,014 km) in all. Many of the officers with whom she was scheduled to visit weren't too pleased that she was coming. However, they were won over by her when they saw not only how pleased the soldiers were with her visit, but by her stamina and good cheer.

In one twelve-hour period, for instance, she inspected two navy hospitals, took a boat to an officers' rest home and had lunch there, returned and inspected an army hospital, reviewed the second Marine Raider Bat-

King George VI, Queen Elizabeth, and First Lady Eleanor Roosevelt in London in 1940

Eleanor shaking hands with a wounded marine in Wellington, New Zealand, in September 1943

On her New Zealand trip, Eleanor rubs noses with a Maori guide in a traditional welcoming gesture.

talion, made a speech at a service club, attended a reception, and was guest of honor at a dinner given by one of the generals.

"When I say that she inspected those hospitals, I don't mean that she shook hands with the chief medical officer, glanced into a sun parlor, and left," wrote one officer. "I mean that she went into every ward, stopped at every bed, and spoke to every patient: What was his name? How did he feel? Was there anything he needed? Could she take a message home for him? I marveled at her hardihood, both physical and mental. She walked for miles

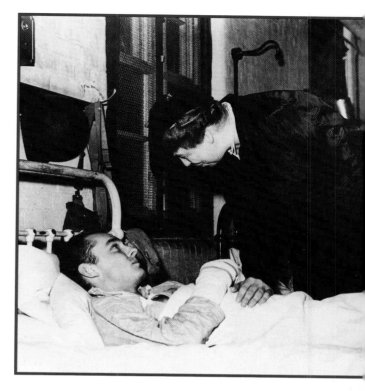

Eleanor speaking to an army staff sergeant at a base hospital somewhere in the British Isles

The First Lady addressing U.S. soldiers in Guadalcanal during World War II

Eleanor with an anti-aircraft unit from Pearl Harbor

On one of her trips during the war, Eleanor joined U.S. soldiers in their mess hall.

and she saw patients who were grievously and gruesomely wounded. But I marveled most at their expressions as she leaned over them." It was a sight, he said, he would never forget.

For Eleanor, the trip was a great success. And yet she was frustrated by what she saw. "If we don't make this a more decent world to live in I don't see how we can look these boys in the eyes," she told a friend after her return. "They're going to fight their handicaps all their lives and what for if the world is the same cruel, stupid place?"

One place she did not think was

Eleanor, on her horse Dot, riding with her son James at Val-Kill

cruel, or stupid, was Val-Kill, her home in Hyde Park, which she visited frequently with both family and friends.

While she was never alone at the White House, it could be a very lonely place. In Hyde Park, she could just be herself with the people she knew and loved.

She spent as much of each summer there as she could, and could always be found knitting when sitting around with guests. She enjoyed reading po-

A Favorite Poem

☆ ☆

Eleanor was an avid reader and writer, and she especially loved poetry. This verse from a poem called "The House by the Side of the Road" by Sam Walter Foss was one of her favorites. A copy of the poem was displayed in the entrance hall at Val-Kill and reveals something about Eleanor's take on life.

> Let me live in a house by the side of the road,
> Where the race of men go by—
> The men who are good and the men who are bad,
> As good and as bad as I.
> I would not sit in the scorner's seat,
> Or hurl the cynic's ban—
> Let me live in a house by the side of the road
> And be a friend to man.

When the king (next to Eleanor) and queen (next to the president) of England visited Hyde Park, Eleanor (left) planned a hot-dog picnic for them at Val-Kill. Franklin's mother Sara is in the center of this picture.

etry out loud as she had years before with Franklin, and often rode her horse Dot in the nearby woods, or swam in her pool or played tennis. She even attempted to ski. "I tried coming down one hill and to everyone's amusement landed in a heap at the bottom," she said.

Even when her official duties spilled over to life at Val-Kill, she kept things casual. When the king and queen of England visited the United States, there was an uproar because Eleanor planned to serve them the most American of foods—hot dogs—at a picnic at Val-Kill. "Oh dear, oh dear, so many people are worried that 'the dignity of our country will be imperiled' by inviting royalty to a picnic, particularly a hot-dog picnic" said Eleanor. "We certainly don't want to make everything so perfectly English that there will be nothing for our guests to smilingly talk about afterwards."

Eleanor loved the summer with her long stays at home and hated for it to end. She missed it when it was gone,

This photograph, taken on January 20, 1945—President Roosevelt's last Inauguration Day—was one of the last group portraits of Franklin and Eleanor with their grandchildren.

explaining that "the tang of fall makes me very sad because it brings the winter and all of its excitement very close . . . someday when I have no longer any obligation to do anything in this world, I am going to be very happy enjoying rural quiet and watching nature carry on its drama of life from the sidelines."

But the sidelines were no place for a woman like Eleanor, not while she was First Lady and not afterward. She knew it, the president knew it, and by now the nation knew it.

☆　☆　☆　☆　☆　☆　☆　☆　☆　☆　☆　☆　☆　☆　☆

CHAPTER SIX

Opportunity Knocks and Keeps Knocking

★ ★ ★ ★ ★ ★ ★ ★ ★ ★ ★ ★ ★ ★

After Franklin's death, Eleanor was urged to do many things—everything from returning to teaching to running for political office herself! But Eleanor wasn't sure what she wanted to do.

"I had few definite plans, but I knew there were certain things I did *not* want to do," she said. "I did not want to run an elaborate household again. I did not want to cease trying to be useful in some way. I did not want to feel old—and I seldom have."

In fact, she delved right back into life soon after moving out of the White House. She became a board member of the National Association for the Advance-

★ ★ ★ ★ ★ ★ ★ ★ ★ ★ ★ ★ ★ ★

Mrs. Roosevelt, one of three United States delegates to the United Nations, listens on earphones to a January 1946 debate in the UN General Assembly.

ment of Colored People (NAACP) and was asked by Franklin's successor, President Harry Truman, to be one of three United States delegates to the newly formed United Nations. This she was especially proud of, as she had long supported its creation. Its first meeting was in London. She called it "one of the most wonderful and worthwhile experiences in my life."

Eleanor continued her work there, speaking out often about human

First Lady of the World

☆ ☆

President Harry Truman called Eleanor Roosevelt "the First Lady of the World" for her many contributions to world peace, social reform, and racial equality. She traveled the globe to see and feel for herself the plight of refugees, the hungry, and the poor. At the root of all her work was her concern for the basic rights of human beings around the world. Everyone, she believed, had a right to freedom of speech and belief and freedom from want and fear. Not surprisingly, one of her proudest achievements came in the early morning hours of December 10, 1948. For two long years, she had served as chairperson of the UN's Human Rights Commission. She and her colleagues worked and argued tirelessly to set down on paper a list of fundamental human rights for all the world to see and enforce. In the wee hours of that December morning, the UN General Assembly approved the Universal Declaration of Human Rights. They then rose to give Eleanor Roosevelt a standing ovation to thank her for her leadership in creating the important document. Indeed, the declaration is Eleanor's living legacy. Today, the declaration guides all dialogue, work, and law regarding the rights everyone around the world should expect to receive.

rights. She debated a Russian Communist leader about whether or not people who fled their homelands should be allowed to return after the war. She continued to fight for civil rights as well. She and her daughter Anna even hosted their own radio show in the late 1940s. A few years later, she and her son Elliott hosted a television talk show featuring such famous guests as Albert Einstein and the Duke and Duchess of Windsor. She also taught at Brandeis University, outside Boston.

Most of all, though, Eleanor Roosevelt never gave up fighting for what she believed in. When President Truman was wavering about whether to

Eleanor Roosevelt in New York City at United Nations headquarters

Eleanor and Margaret Truman at a 1949 UN General Assembly meeting

Eleanor (right) escaping a rain shower in Sendai, Japan, during a 1953 trip

support the creation of the State of Israel, for instance, she threatened to quit her United Nations post if he did not support the new state. He did support Israel and she did stay. When the next president after Truman was elected, however, he was a Republican, and she did leave the United Nations. She returned in 1961, when President John F. Kennedy reap-

A 1954 photograph of Eleanor with her four sons

pointed her. She was almost eighty years old at the time.

As always, Eleanor traveled constantly. In the 1950s alone, she went to Israel three times, Japan twice, to Europe many, many times, as well as to South America, Indonesia, Iran, Turkey, Thailand, and Russia. "For some time now, my children and my friends have been warning me that I must slow down," she said when she was already an old woman. "I am willing to slow down but I just don't know how." In 1962, she contracted a rare blood disease and died November 7 in New York City.

"I have never been bored, never found the days long enough for the range of activities with which I wanted to fill them," Eleanor once wrote. As America's most popular First Lady, Eleanor Roosevelt rose above the constraints that had held back others, both as a human being and as the president's wife. She spoke out for what she believed and she worked to achieve her goals. No other First Lady before her or since has done as much. Few, it seems, have even tried.

Profile of America, 1962: We Shall Overcome

✫ ✫

At Eleanor's death in 1962, President John F. Kennedy's administration was in full bloom. Kennedy was the youngest president yet to hold office, and his youthful enthusiasm inspired a generation. He awakened the country from its sleepy contentment of the 1950s to a new sense of commitment, idealism, and optimism. His brief presidency is often called "Camelot," after the charmed court of King Arthur. In 1962, Kennedy's assassination was a year away, and Americans believed that all things were possible.

Eleanor might have been cheered by the growing enthusiasm of America's youth toward reform, civil rights, and social action. Kennedy's spirited efforts to energize the nation, enliven a sluggish economy, support the arts and education, and improve human rights inspired people to join in. The civil-rights movement gathered steam. In the fall, federal officers escorted James Meredith to classes at the University of Mississippi. As the first African-American person to attend the school, his enrollment caused riots and controversy, but Meredith earned his degree.

At the same time, America faced a crisis in Cuba over missile bases the Soviets were building there. American leaders believed that the missiles threatened national security. Unable to come to terms, America and the Soviet Union hurtled toward nuclear war. Even though the Soviet Union backed down at the last minute, the close call shook both President Kennedy and Soviet premier Nikita Khrushchev. The two agreed to establish a "hotline," a special phone line to use in emergencies. It was a positive step toward improving communication between the two Cold War enemies.

The Soviets challenged the United States in the "space race" as well. They were first to launch a man into earth orbit. In 1962, astronaut John Glenn became the first American to orbit the earth, circling three times. Glenn became a true American hero, and the word "splashdown" entered the English language.

The Beatles, the hippies, the war protests, and miniskirts were several years away. Mohammed Ali was still Cassius Clay. The "mod" look, with its loud colors and geometric patterns, would come later. In 1962, women still favored the conservative sweaters, skirts, and elegant fashions made popular by Jackie Kennedy. Men wore their hair short, and girls puffed theirs up into "bouffants" and "beehives." Everyone loved the Beach Boys, diet colas, TV, and Elizabeth Taylor. Basketball star Wilt Chamberlain scored 100 points for Philadelphia in a game against New York.

Amid the optimism, hints of coming problems began to surface. Folksinger Bob Dylan's song of the year, "Blowin' in the Wind," expressed despair over social injustice. In her book *Silent Spring*, Rachel Carson warned for the first time against the dangers of insecticides. More and more American military advisers and supplies were sent to Vietnam. Despite what lay ahead, however, Americans in 1962 believed they could overcome.

* * * * * * * * * * * * * * * *

The Presidents and Their First Ladies

President	Birth–Death	First Lady	Birth–Death
YEARS IN OFFICE			
1789–1797			
George Washington	1732–1799	Martha Dandridge Custis Washington	1731–1802
1797–1801			
John Adams	1735–1826	Abigail Smith Adams	1744–1818
1801–1809			
Thomas Jefferson†	1743–1826		
1809–1817			
James Madison	1751–1836	Dolley Payne Todd Madison	1768–1849
1817–1825			
James Monroe	1758–1831	Elizabeth Kortright Monroe	1768–1830
1825–1829			
John Quincy Adams	1767–1848	Louisa Catherine Johnson Adams	1775–1852
1829–1837			
Andrew Jackson†	1767–1845		
1837–1841			
Martin Van Buren†	1782–1862		
1841			
William Henry Harrison‡	1773–1841		
1841–1845			
John Tyler	1790–1862	Letitia Christian Tyler (1841–1842)	1790–1842
		Julia Gardiner Tyler (1844–1845)	1820–1889
1845–1849			
James K. Polk	1795–1849	Sarah Childress Polk	1803–1891
1849–1850			
Zachary Taylor	1784–1850	Margaret Mackall Smith Taylor	1788–1852
1850–1853			
Millard Fillmore	1800–1874	Abigail Powers Fillmore	1798–1853
1853–1857			
Franklin Pierce	1804–1869	Jane Means Appleton Pierce	1806–1863
1857–1861			
James Buchanan*	1791–1868		
1861–1865			
Abraham Lincoln	1809–1865	Mary Todd Lincoln	1818–1882
1865–1869			
Andrew Johnson	1808–1875	Eliza McCardle Johnson	1810–1876
1869–1877			
Ulysses S. Grant	1822–1885	Julia Dent Grant	1826–1902
1877–1881			
Rutherford B. Hayes	1822–1893	Lucy Ware Webb Hayes	1831–1889
1881			
James A. Garfield	1831–1881	Lucretia Rudolph Garfield	1832–1918
1881–1885			
Chester A. Arthur†	1829–1886		

† wife died before he took office   ‡ wife too ill to accompany him to Washington   * never married

1885–1889			
Grover Cleveland	1837–1908	Frances Folsom Cleveland	1864–1947
1889–1893			
Benjamin Harrison	1833–1901	Caroline Lavinia Scott Harrison	1832–1892
1893–1897			
Grover Cleveland	1837–1908	Frances Folsom Cleveland	1864–1947
1897–1901			
William McKinley	1843–1901	Ida Saxton McKinley	1847–1907
1901–1909			
Theodore Roosevelt	1858–1919	Edith Kermit Carow Roosevelt	1861–1948
1909–1913			
William Howard Taft	1857–1930	Helen Herron Taft	1861–1943
1913–1921			
Woodrow Wilson	1856–1924	Ellen Louise Axson Wilson (1913–1914)	1860–1914
		Edith Bolling Galt Wilson (1915–1921)	1872–1961
1921–1923			
Warren G. Harding	1865–1923	Florence Kling Harding	1860–1924
1923–1929			
Calvin Coolidge	1872–1933	Grace Anna Goodhue Coolidge	1879–1957
1929–1933			
Herbert Hoover	1874–1964	Lou Henry Hoover	1874–1944
1933–1945			
Franklin D. Roosevelt	1882–1945	Anna Eleanor Roosevelt	1884–1962
1945–1953			
Harry S. Truman	1884–1972	Bess Wallace Truman	1885–1982
1953–1961			
Dwight D. Eisenhower	1890–1969	Mamie Geneva Doud Eisenhower	1896–1979
1961–1963			
John F. Kennedy	1917–1963	Jacqueline Bouvier Kennedy	1929–1994
1963–1969			
Lyndon B. Johnson	1908–1973	Claudia Taylor (Lady Bird) Johnson	1912–
1969–1974			
Richard Nixon	1913–1994	Patricia Ryan Nixon	1912–1993
1974–1977			
Gerald Ford	1913–	Elizabeth Bloomer Ford	1918–
1977–1981			
James Carter	1924–	Rosalynn Smith Carter	1927–
1981–1989			
Ronald Reagan	1911–	Nancy Davis Reagan	1923–
1989–1993			
George Bush	1924–	Barbara Pierce Bush	1925–
1993–			
William Jefferson Clinton	1946–	Hillary Rodham Clinton	1947–

Anna Eleanor Roosevelt Timeline

1884	★	Anna Eleanor Roosevelt is born
		Grover Cleveland is elected president
1888	★	Benjamin Harrison is elected president
1892	★	Ellis Island immigration center opens
		Grover Cleveland is elected president
1893	★	Woman suffrage is adopted in Colorado
		Economic depression hits the United States
1896	★	William McKinley is elected president
1898	★	Spanish-American War is fought, resulting in the United States annexing Puerto Rico, Guam, and the Philippines
1900	★	William McKinley is reelected president
1901	★	President McKinley is assassinated
		Theodore Roosevelt becomes president
1904	★	Theodore Roosevelt is elected president
1905	★	Eleanor Roosevelt marries Franklin D. Roosevelt
1906	★	Anna Eleanor Roosevelt is born
		Theodore Roosevelt receives the Nobel Peace Prize
1907	★	James Roosevelt is born
1908	★	William Howard Taft is elected president
1909	★	National Association for the Advancement of Colored People (NAACP) is founded
		Third child, Franklin Roosevelt, is born and dies almost eight months later
1910	★	Boy Scouts of America is founded
		Elliott Roosevelt is born
		Franklin D. Roosevelt is elected to New York senate

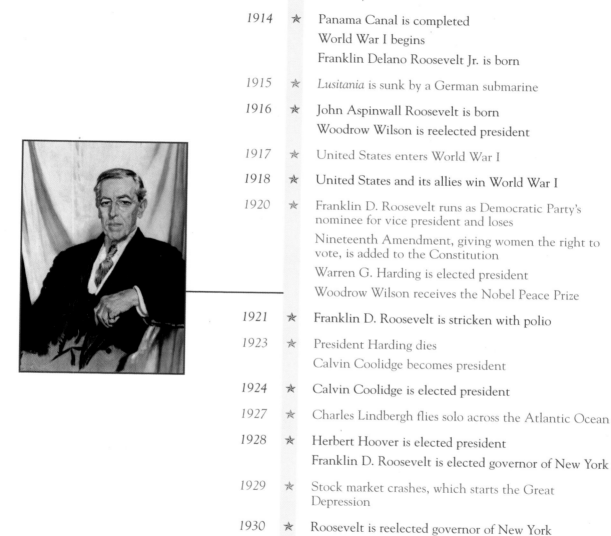

1912	★	Woodrow Wilson is elected president
		Titanic sinks in the North Atlantic
1913	★	Henry Ford sets up his first assembly line
		Franklin D. Roosevelt becomes assistant secretary of the navy
1914	★	Panama Canal is completed
		World War I begins
		Franklin Delano Roosevelt Jr. is born
1915	★	*Lusitania* is sunk by a German submarine
1916	★	John Aspinwall Roosevelt is born
		Woodrow Wilson is reelected president
1917	★	United States enters World War I
1918	★	United States and its allies win World War I
1920	★	Franklin D. Roosevelt runs as Democratic Party's nominee for vice president and loses
		Nineteenth Amendment, giving women the right to vote, is added to the Constitution
		Warren G. Harding is elected president
		Woodrow Wilson receives the Nobel Peace Prize
1921	★	Franklin D. Roosevelt is stricken with polio
1923	★	President Harding dies
		Calvin Coolidge becomes president
1924	★	Calvin Coolidge is elected president
1927	★	Charles Lindbergh flies solo across the Atlantic Ocean
1928	★	Herbert Hoover is elected president
		Franklin D. Roosevelt is elected governor of New York
1929	★	Stock market crashes, which starts the Great Depression
1930	★	Roosevelt is reelected governor of New York
1931	★	"The Star-Spangled Banner" becomes the national anthem
		Banks fail across the country

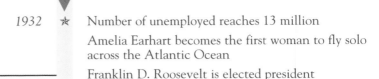

1932	★	Number of unemployed reaches 13 million
		Amelia Earhart becomes the first woman to fly solo across the Atlantic Ocean
		Franklin D. Roosevelt is elected president
1933	★	President Roosevelt begins the New Deal
		Civilian Conservation Corps (CCC) is established
		Tennessee Valley Authority Act (TVA) is signed
		Banking Act of 1933 is signed
1934	★	Number of unemployed is 9 million
		Securities and Exchange Commission is established
1935	★	Congress passes the Social Security Act
		Works Progress Administration (WPA) is established
		Rural Electrification Administration (REA) is established
1936	★	Franklin D. Roosevelt is reelected president
1939	★	World War II begins
1940	★	Selective Service Act is signed
		Franklin D. Roosevelt is reelected president
1941	★	Japanese bomb Pearl Harbor
		President Roosevelt asks for a declaration of war; United States enters World War II
1942	★	President Roosevelt signs executive order to intern persons of Japanese descent
		Philippines is captured by Japanese
		U.S. forces win Battle of Midway
		U.S. troops land in North Africa
1943	★	U.S. and British forces invade Italy
		Food rationing begins
		President Roosevelt attends conferences with leaders of the Allies in Cairo and Tehran
1944	★	Allies stage the D-Day invasion at Normandy, France
		Philippines is liberated
		Franklin D. Roosevelt is reelected president
		Allies suffer heavy losses in Battle of the Bulge

1945	★	President Roosevelt attends Yalta Conference with other Allied leaders
		President Roosevelt dies
		Harry S. Truman becomes president
		Germany surrenders to the Allies in Europe
		United States drops atomic bombs on Japan
		Japan surrenders, ending World War II
		Eleanor Roosevelt is appointed a delegate to the General Assembly of the United Nations
1947	★	**Truman Doctrine extends aid to Greece and Turkey**
1948	★	Marshall Plan extends aid to war-torn Europe
		Berlin Airlift begins
		Harry S. Truman is elected president
		The Universal Declaration of Human Rights is adopted by the General Assembly of the United Nations
1949	★	**United Nations headquarters is dedicated in New York City**
1950	★	President Truman sends U.S. forces to fight in Korean War
1952	★	**Dwight D. Eisenhower is elected president**
1953	★	Korean War ends
1954	★	Supreme Court declares segregated schools to be unconstitutional
1956	★	Dwight D. Eisenhower is reelected president
1960	★	**John F. Kennedy is elected president**
		Civil Rights Act of 1960 is passed
1961	★	First Americans fly in space
		United States sends aid and advisors to South Vietnam
		Peace Corps is established
1962	★	President Kennedy forces Soviet Union to remove missiles from Cuba
		Anna Eleanor Roosevelt dies on November 7

101

Fast Facts about
Anna Eleanor Roosevelt

Born: October 11, 1884, in New York City

Died: November 7, 1962, in New York City

Burial Site: Hyde Park, New York

Parents: Elliott Roosevelt and Anna Eleanor Livingston Hall Roosevelt

Education: Private tutors; Allenswood Boarding School in England

Careers: Volunteer work with Junior League, Consumers League, Red Cross; teacher at Todhunter, a girls' school; newspaper columnist; U.S. delegate to the United Nations; host of a television show; teacher at Brandeis University

Marriage: March 17, 1905, to Franklin D. Roosevelt until his death on April 12, 1945

Children: Anna Eleanor Roosevelt, James Roosevelt, Franklin Roosevelt (March 18–November 8, 1909), Elliott Roosevelt, Franklin Delano Roosevelt Jr., John Aspinwall Roosevelt

Places She Lived: New York City (1884–1891, 1902–1911, 1920–1929, 1945–1962); Tivoli, New York (1891–1899); England (1899–1902); Albany, New York (1911–1913, 1929–1933); Washington, D.C. (1913–1920, 1933–1945); Hyde Park, New York (1925–1962)

Major Achievements:

 ✯ Worked to promote racial equality by making speeches against segregation in the South, recommending desegregation of the armed forces, and by resigning from the DAR when they refused to let African-American Marian Anderson sing in their building (1939).

 ✯ Founded Americans for Democratic Action (1945) and became a board member of the NAACP.

 ✯ Served as U.S. delegate to the General Assembly of the United Nations (1945, 1947–1952, 1961).

 ✯ Chaired the UN commission that wrote the Universal Declaration of Human Rights (adopted in 1948).

 ✯ Wrote a newspaper column "My Day"(1936) and authored twenty-three books, including *It's Up to the Women* (1933), *This I Remember* (1949), and *Tomorrow Is Now* (1963).

Fast Facts about Franklin Delano Roosevelt's Presidency

Terms of Office: Elected in 1932; reelected in 1936, 1940, and 1944; served as the thirty-second president of the United States from 1933 until his death on April 12, 1945; the only president to be elected to more than two terms of office.

Vice Presidents: John Nance Garner (1933–1941); Henry Agard Wallace (1941–1945); Harry S. Truman (January 20, 1945, to April 12, 1945).

Major Decisions and Legislation:
* Declared a bank holiday to help the banking industry recover (1933).
* Signed New Deal legislation (1933) to help end the depression, including the Civilian Conservation Corps Reconstruction Relief Act, the Federal Emergency Relief Act, the Tennessee Valley Authority Act, the Federal Securities Act, and the National Industrial Recovery Act.
* Signed the Social Security and Railroad Retirement Acts (1935).
* Signed the Lend-Lease Act (March 1941) to help Britain fight Germany during World War II.
* Asked Congress to declare war after Japan bombed Pearl Harbor (1941) and brought the United States into World War II on the side of the Allies.

Major Events:
* Franklin D. Roosevelt was the first and only president elected to a third and then a fourth term of office (1940, 1944).
* The Twenty-first Amendment, which repealed the Eighteenth Amendment by overturning Prohibition, was added to the U.S. Constitution (1933).
* Appointed Frances Perkins secretary of labor, the first woman to hold a cabinet post, and Ruth Bryan Owen as a minister to Denmark and Iceland, the first woman to represent the United States in another country.
* Made the following appointments to the U.S. Supreme Court: Chief Justice Harlan Stone (1941); Associate Justices Hugo Black (1937), Stanley Reed (1938), Felix Frankfurter and William Douglas (1939), Frank Murphy (1940), James Francis Byrnes and Robert Jackson (1941), and Wiley Rutledge (1943).
* The United States enters World War II on the side of the Allies (1941).

Where to Visit

The Capitol Building
Constitution Avenue
Washington, D.C. 20510
(202) 225-3121

The Franklin D. Roosevelt Library and
    Museum
511 Albany Post Road
Hyde Park, New York 12538-1999
Phone: (914) 229-8114
Fax: (914) 229-0872

Home of Franklin D. Roosevelt
    National Historic Site
519 Albany Post Road
Hyde Park, New York 12538
(914) 229-9115

Museum of American History of the
    Smithsonian Institution "First
    Ladies: Political and Public Image"
14th St. and Constitution Avenue NW
Washington, D.C.
(202) 357-2008

National Archives
Constitution Avenue
Washington, D.C. 20408
(202) 501-5000

The National First Ladies Library
The Saxton McKinley House
331 South Market Avenue
Canton, Ohio 44702

White House
1600 Pennsylvania Avenue
Washington, D.C. 20500
Visitor's Office: (202) 456-7041

White House Historical Association
740 Jackson Place NW
Washington, D.C. 20503
(202) 737-8292

Online Sites of Interest

The First Ladies of the United States of America

http://www2.whitehouse.gov/WH/glimpse/firstladies/html/firstladies.html

A portrait and biography of each First Lady; links to other White House sites.

Franklin D. Roosevelt Library and Museum

http://www.academic.marist.edu/fdr/

Located in Hyde Park, New York, it is part of a system of presidential libraries. Two wings are devoted to the memory of Eleanor Roosevelt. Includes descriptions, pictures, and thousands of online, copyright-free photos.

Home of Franklin D. Roosevelt National Historic Site

http://www.nps.gov/hofr/

Called Springwood, the home is next to the Franklin D. Roosevelt Library and Museum. Includes information on tours, exhibits, lodging, fees, and more.

Internet Public Library, Presidents of the United States (IPL POTUS)

http://www.ipl.org/ref/POTUS/fdroosevelt.html

Much information on FDR, including personal information and facts about his presidency; many links to other sites including biographies and other Internet resources.

The National First Ladies Library

http://www.firstladies.org

The first virtual library devoted to the lives and legacies of America's First Ladies; includes a bibliography of material by and about the First Ladies and a tour of the Saxton McKinley House in Canton, Ohio, which houses the library.

The Universal Declaration of Human Rights (50th Anniversary)

http://www.mcmun.org/1998/hr/index.html

Information on the 50th anniversary of the declaration; includes a link to the text, which was created and adopted when Eleanor Roosevelt was chairperson of the UN Human Rights Commission and is her most important legacy.

The White House

http://www.whitehouse.gov/WH/Welcome.html

Information about the current president and vice president; White House history and tours; biographies of past presidents and their families; a tour of the historic building, current events, and much more.

For Further Reading

Faber, Doris. *Eleanor Roosevelt: First Lady of the World*. Women of Our Time. New York: Puffin Books, 1996.

Freedman, Russell. *Eleanor Roosevelt: A Life of Discovery*. New York: Clarion Books, 1997.

Gormley, Beatrice. *First Ladies*. New York: Scholastic, Inc., 1997.

Gottfried, Ted. *Eleanor Roosevelt: First Lady of the Twentieth Century*. Book Report Biographies. Danbury, Conn.: Franklin Watts, 1997.

Gould, Lewis L. (ed.). *American First Ladies: Their Lives and Their Legacy*. New York: Garland Publishing, 1996.

Mayo, Edith P. (ed.). *The Smithsonian Book of the First Ladies: Their Lives, Times, and Issues*. New York: Henry Holt, 1996.

McGowen, Tom. *World War II*. New York: Franklin Watts, 1993.

Osinski, Alice. *Franklin D. Roosevelt: Thirty-second President of the United States*. Chicago: Childrens Press, 1987.

Shebar, Sharon. *Franklin D. Roosevelt and the New Deal*. Henry Steele Commager's Americans. New York: Barrons Juveniles, 1987.

Spangenburg, Ray. *Eleanor Roosevelt: A Passion to Improve*. Makers of America. New York: Facts on File, 1997.

Stein, R. Conrad. *The Great Depression*. Cornerstones of Freedom. Chicago: Childrens Press, 1993.

Stewart, Gail. *The New Deal*. Parsippany, N. J.: New Discovery Books, 1993.

Sullivan, George. *The Day the Women Got the Vote: A Photo History of the Women's Rights Movement*. New York: Scholastic Inc., 1994.

Toor, Rachel. *Eleanor Roosevelt*. American Women of Achievement. New York: Chelsea House Publishing, 1989.

Vercelli, Jane Anderson. *Eleanor Roosevelt*. Junior World Biographies. New York: Chelsea House Publishing, 1995.

Weidt, Maryann N. *Stateswoman to the World: A Story about Eleanor Roosevelt*. Minneapolis: Carolrhoda Books, Inc., 1991.

Weil, Ann. *Eleanor Roosevelt: Fighter for Social Justice*. The Childhood of Famous Americans. New York: Aladdin Paperbacks, 1989.

Index

Page numbers in **boldface type** indicate illustrations

Photo Identifications

Cover: Detail of Douglas Chandor portrait of Eleanor Roosevelt at age sixty-five
Page 8: Full-length formal portrait of Eleanor Roosevelt photographed by Edward Steichen for Vogue
Page 22: Eleanor Roosevelt at the age of four
Page 38: Eleanor in her wedding dress
Page 50: Eleanor Roosevelt with her first child, Anna
Page 66: Douglas Chandor portrait of Eleanor Roosevelt at age sixty-five
Page 88: A head-and-shoulders photograph of Eleanor Roosevelt

Photo Credits©

About the Author

Dan Santow is a former producer of "The Oprah Winfrey Show" and writer at *People* magazine. He is the author of *The Irreverent Guide: Chicago* (Frommer's/Macmillan, 1996) and has been published in many magazines, including *Redbook, Town & Country, Metropolitan Home, Men's Health, Chicago* magazine, the *Chicago Tribune Magazine*, and *Advertising Age*, among others. Mr. Santow is a graduate of Vassar College and holds a master's degree in journalism from Northwestern University. He lives in Chicago.